A FAIRY TALE FOR GROWN-UP CHILDREN

India, Company School, circa 1870, gouache on paper.

LOVE

A FAIRY TALE FOR GROWN-UP CHILDREN

BY OSCAR A.Z. LENEMAN

PHOTOGRAPHY BY LEE BOLTIN

All the antique paintings shown
in this fairy tale were assembled
by Lenem'Arts Inc. of New York.

COLUMBUS BOOKS

and

Morgan & Morgan

1983

U.S. and Canada

Published by Morgan & Morgan, Inc.
145 Palisade Street
Dobbs Ferry, New York 10522

International Standard Book Number (paper) 0-87100-193-4
International Standard Book Number (cloth) 0-87100-198-5
Library of Congress Catalog Card Number 83-62549

International Edition excluding U.S. and Canada

Published by Columbus Books
Devonshire House
29 Elmfield Road
Bromley, Kent, BR1 1LT

International Standard Book Number 0-86287-051-8

Printed in U.S.A. by Morgan Press, Dobbs Ferry, New York.
Book Design by John O'Mara

For Nina

Once upon a time. . .

India, Natdwara School, circa 1900, gouache on paper.

a young princess was dreaming and waiting for
her prince charming to ride by on a white horse.

India, Moghul/Deccan School, circa 1730, gouache on paper.

Meanwhile, she ignored all other suitors,
including those on birds,

and those on foot,

Japan, late 19th century, gouache on paper.

as she consoled herself with a daikon.

India, Natdwara School, circa 1870, gouache on paper.

Spring fever was in the air and everyone was getting friendlier.

India, Rajput School, 19th century, gouache on paper.

Japan, 19th century, woodcut.

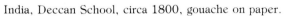
India, Deccan School, circa 1800, gouache on paper.

One blissful day the princess looked up . . .

India, Jaipur School, circa 1840, gouache on paper.

and there was her prince charming riding by
on his white horse!

India, Bikaner School, circa 1780, gouache on paper.

After her toilette . . .

India, Bikaner School, circa 1780, gouache on paper.

she went to the prince's court for her
coming out party.

Japan, 19th century, gouache on silk.

That evening, after some sake,

Japan, 19th century, woodblock print.

and some footsie,

Thailand, 19th century, gouache on paper.

the prince dragged her into the bushes . . .

Japan, 19th century, woodblock print.

for a sweet kiss,

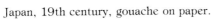
Japan, 19th century, gouache on paper.

and a gentle blow.

More frolic...

Japan, 19th century, woodblock print.

and more kisses led to the music.

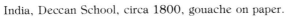

India, Deccan School, circa 1800, gouache on paper.

"Voulez-vous coucher avec moi ce soir?"

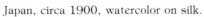
Japan, circa 1900, watercolor on silk.

Licking his chops,

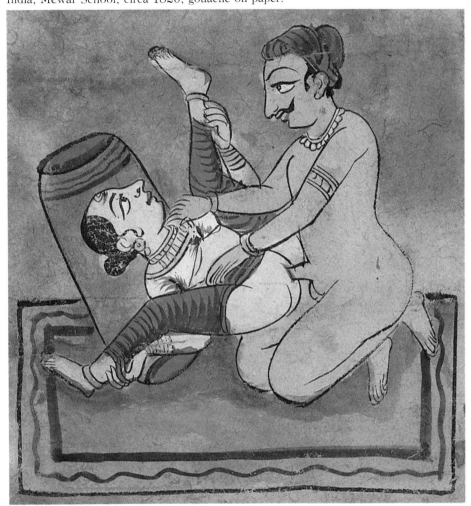

the prince expressed his deep affection,

China, 19th century, watercolor on paper.

reassuring her of his unbending love, on . . .

India, Deccan School, circa 1800, gouache on paper.

and on . . .

Japan, 19th century, pen and ink on paper.

and on . . .

Japan, circa 1900, watercolor on silk.

and on . . .

Japan, 19th century, pen and ink on paper.

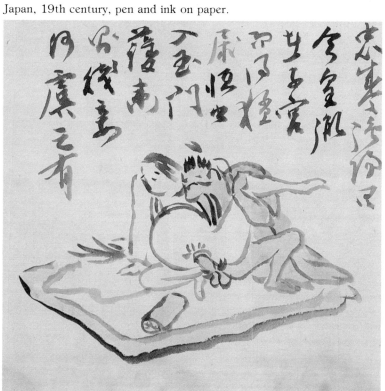

and on . . .

Japan, 19th century, pen and ink on paper.

and on . . .

China, 19th century, watercolor on paper.

and on . . .

Japan, 19th century, watercolor on silk.

and on . . .

climaxing in a tantric explosion...

India, Rajput School, 20th century, gouache on paper.

of cosmic love.

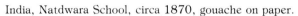
India, Natdwara School, circa 1870, gouache on paper.

In the days that followed, palace life was festive.

Indochina, circa 1900, pen and ink drawing.

The streets were swept.

India, Marwar School, circa 1860, gouache on paper.

Everyone was decked out in
his best finery . . .

India, Tanjore School, circa 1840, gouache on paper.

and jewels.

Indochina, circa 1900, pen and ink drawing.

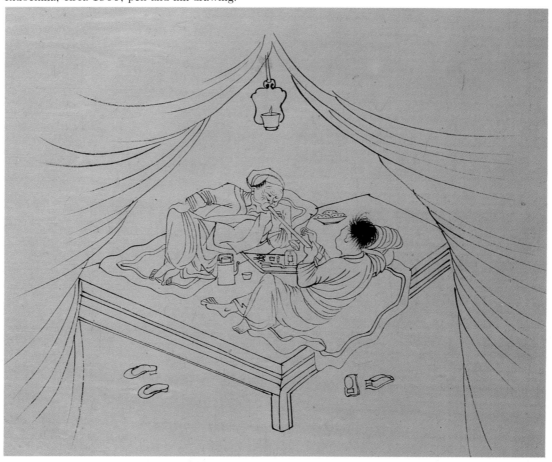

Euphoria prevailed . . .

and champagne flowed.

India, Marwar School, circa 1840, gouache on paper.

Deals were made,

queries were openly aired,

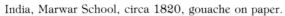
India, Marwar School, circa 1820, gouache on paper.

and tigers had the day of their lives.

One day . . .

China, 19th century, watercolor on paper.

while having a french lesson,

India, Mewar School, circa 1790, gouache on paper.

the prince came upon the expression
"Ménage à trois."

Japan, 19th century, watercolor on paper.

He requested an immediate demonstration,

China, 19th century, watercolor on paper.

which went on . . .

India, Mewar School, circa 1800, gouache on paper.

and on . . .

Japan, 19th century, woodblock print.

and on . . .

India, Rajput School, circa 1840, gouache on paper.

As the prince got carried away
with his new frivolities,

India, Marwar School, circa 1860, gouache on paper.

all this macho macho was
beginning to get to the princess.

India-Persia, 19th century, gouache on paper.

"What's good for the gander is good for the goose,"
whispered her best friend in confidence...

Japan, 19th century, woodcut by Kunisada.

and suddenly extra helping hands volunteered. . . .

Japan, 19th century, woodblock print.

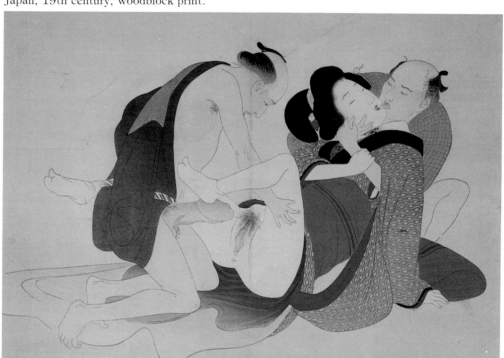

and on . . .

Japan, 19th century, watercolor on paper.

and on . . .

India, Jaipur School, circa 1840, gouache on paper.

'Midst all this bliss, the princess
adopted a little puppy. . .

India, Natdwara School, circa 1860, gouache on paper.

much to the enchantment of the prince.

India, Mewar School, circa 1800, gouache on paper.

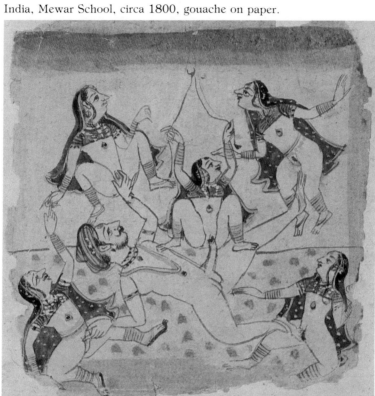

They went around the world,

India, Marwar School, circa 1780, gouache on paper.

did some acrobatics. . .

India, Rajput School, circa 1850, gouache on paper.

and lived happily ever after.